**Te**

# Excel 2010 Pivot Tables

Tim Hill

*Questing Vole Press*

*Excel 2010 Pivot Tables (Tech 102)*
by Tim Hill

Editor: Kevin Debenjak
Proofreader: Janet Ott
Compositor: Kim Frees
Cover Illustrator: Rayne Beaudoin
Cover: Questing Vole Press


Version 14.0.6

# Contents

# 1                            Pivot Table Basics

You can use Excel's **pivot tables** to quickly create concise, flexible summaries of long lists of raw values, without having to write new formulas, copy and paste cells, or reorganize rows and columns. Pivot tables are **dynamic**: if you create a pivot table from, say, census data, then you can drag your mouse to rearrange the table so that it summarizes any variables of interest—age, gender, location, education, income, and so on. Rearranging a pivot table by swapping or moving rows and columns is called **pivoting**: turning the same information to view it at different angles. The jargon associated with pivot tables ("*n*-dimensional cross tabulations") makes them look complex, but they're really no more than an easy way to build flexible summary tables.

Excel offers other features for analyzing large amounts of data—such as outlines, automatic subtotals, and statistical functions—but if you're working with hundreds (or hundreds of thousands) of rows, then pivot tables are the best way to look at the same information in different ways, summarize data on the fly, and spot trends and relationships.

## Downloading the Sample Workbook

To create a pivot table, you need a long list of raw data values to summarize. (A short list works too but doesn't show the real power of pivot tables.) To follow along with the examples in this book, download the Excel workbook **orders.xlsx** from *questingvolepress.com*. In orders.xlsx, the worksheet named Source Data contains a list of 2155 records (rows) from grocery-item orders.

| | A | B | C | D | E | F | G | H | I |
|---|---|---|---|---|---|---|---|---|---|
| 1 | Order ID | Product | Category | Unit Price | Quantity | Customer | Ship City | Ship Country | Order Date |
| 2 | 10248 | Singaporean Hokkien Fried Mee | Grains/Cereals | 9.8 | 10 | Vins et alcools Chevalier | Reims | France | 04-Aug-94 |
| 3 | 10248 | Mozzarella di Giovanni | Dairy Products | 34.8 | 5 | Vins et alcools Chevalier | Reims | France | 04-Aug-94 |
| 4 | 10248 | Queso Cabrales | Dairy Products | 14 | 12 | Vins et alcools Chevalier | Reims | France | 04-Aug-94 |
| 5 | 10249 | Tofu | Produce | 18.6 | 9 | Toms Spezialitäten | Münster | Germany | 05-Aug-94 |
| 6 | 10249 | Manjimup Dried Apples | Produce | 42.4 | 40 | Toms Spezialitäten | Münster | Germany | 05-Aug-94 |
| 7 | 10250 | Louisiana Fiery Hot Pepper Sauce | Condiments | 16.8 | 15 | Hanari Carnes | Rio de Janeiro | Brazil | 08-Aug-94 |
| 8 | 10250 | Jack's New England Clam Chowder | Seafood | 7.7 | 10 | Hanari Carnes | Rio de Janeiro | Brazil | 08-Aug-94 |
| 9 | 10250 | Manjimup Dried Apples | Produce | 42.4 | 35 | Hanari Carnes | Rio de Janeiro | Brazil | 08-Aug-94 |
| 10 | 10251 | Louisiana Fiery Hot Pepper Sauce | Condiments | 16.8 | 20 | Victuailles en stock | Lyon | France | 08-Aug-94 |
| 11 | 10251 | Gustaf's Knäckebröd | Grains/Cereals | 16.8 | 6 | Victuailles en stock | Lyon | France | 08-Aug-94 |
| 12 | 10251 | Ravioli Angelo | Grains/Cereals | 15.6 | 15 | Victuailles en stock | Lyon | France | 08-Aug-94 |
| 13 | 10252 | Sir Rodney's Marmalade | Confections | 64.8 | 40 | Suprêmes délices | Charleroi | Belgium | 09-Aug-94 |
| 14 | 10252 | Geitost | Dairy Products | 2 | 25 | Suprêmes délices | Charleroi | Belgium | 09-Aug-94 |
| 15 | 10252 | Camembert Pierrot | Dairy Products | 27.2 | 40 | Suprêmes délices | Charleroi | Belgium | 09-Aug-94 |
| 16 | 10253 | Maxilaku | Confections | 16 | 40 | Hanari Carnes | Rio de Janeiro | Brazil | 10-Aug-94 |
| 17 | 10253 | Chartreuse verte | Beverages | 14.4 | 42 | Hanari Carnes | Rio de Janeiro | Brazil | 10-Aug-94 |
| 18 | 10253 | Gorgonzola Telino | Dairy Products | 10 | 20 | Hanari Carnes | Rio de Janeiro | Brazil | 10-Aug-94 |
| 19 | 10254 | Pâté chinois | Meat/Poultry | 19.2 | 21 | Chop-suey Chinese | Bern | Switzerland | 11-Aug-94 |
| 20 | 10254 | Longlife Tofu | Produce | 8 | 21 | Chop-suey Chinese | Bern | Switzerland | 11-Aug-94 |

# Data Requirements for Pivot Tables

Pivot tables let you make comparisons and answer specific questions. To work well with pivot tables, a data list needs to meet the following criteria.

*At least one column has duplicate values*

Pivot tables are used to divide a list into logical **levels** (categories) and calculate statistics for each level. In the sample orders list, the column Customer, for example, has multiple records with the same value (denoting repeat customers). You can summarize the items ordered by each customer where each distinct customer is one level. In real-life data, the number of distinct values in a categorical column ranges from a few (gender or marital status, for example) to a few hundred (geographic location or part number); beyond a few hundred distinct values, analysis becomes unwieldy unless you group (Chapter 3) or filter (Chapter 5) categories.

*At least one column has numerical values*

Numerical values are used to calculate statistics (sum, count, average, maximum, percentage, rank, custom formula, and more) for each column and level of interest. For non-numerical columns, the only statistics that you can calculate are frequency tabulations (page 59): counts of the number of levels (distinct values) in the column. For details about calculating statistics, see Chapter 4.

## Sample Workbook Columns

The orders list in the sample workbook (page 1) contains the following columns.

*Order ID*

Categorical. Identifies an order uniquely. An order for multiple products spans multiple rows. Order 10248, for example, spans rows 2, 3, and 4 (one product per row). Though the order IDs are numbers (10248, 10249,…), this column is actually categorical because it makes no sense to do mathematical operations on its values (summing IDs is meaningless, for example).

*Product*

Categorical. The brand name of the ordered product (Jack's New England Clam Chowder, Manjimup Dried Apples, and so on).

*Category*

Categorical. The type of the ordered product (Seafood, Produce, and so on).

*Unit Price*

Numerical. The selling price of a single unit of the ordered product.

*Quantity*

Numerical. The number of units of the product sold in the order.

*Customer*

Categorical. The name of the buyer.

*Ship City*

Categorical. The city (in Ship Country) where the order was shipped.

*Ship Country*

Categorical. The country where the order was shipped.

*Order Date*

Categorical. The date that the order was placed.

## Creating Pivot Tables

To create a new pivot table, you run the Create PivotTable wizard, which lets you select the data to summarize and position the pivot table on a worksheet. You can then structure the pivot table and organize and filter your data however you like.

### To create a pivot table:

1   Select the range of cells (including column titles) that you want to use for the pivot table. Alternatively, select a single cell in the range and Excel will expand the range automatically; if Excel misidentifies the range, you can fix it in the next step.

It's actually preferable to use a *table* (Insert tab > Tables group > Table, or press Ctrl+T) instead of selecting a range of cells. That way, Excel automatically accounts for any new rows that you add to the source data when you refresh the pivot table (page 12). If you use a range instead of a table, then you must redefine the data source if you add new rows to the end of the range (PivotTable Tools > Options tab > Data group > Change Data Source).

2   Choose Insert tab > Tables group > PivotTable.

Alternatively, if you're creating a pivot table for a table that you defined with Insert tab > Tables group > Table, then you can click anywhere inside the table and then choose Table Tools > Design tab > Tools group > Summarize with PivotTable.

The Create PivotTable dialog box opens. Excel automatically chooses "Select a table or range", with the table name or cell range that you selected. (To create a pivot table based on an external database, you must first configure your database as an external data source: choose Data tab > Connections group.)

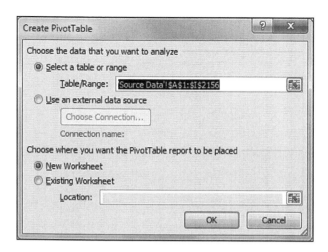

**3** Select "New Worksheet" to create a new worksheet for the pivot table (typically the best option).

Alternatively, choose "Existing Worksheet" to insert the pivot table on a worksheet that's already in your workbook. Specify the cell reference for the top-left corner of the pivot table. Excel overwrites any values in the target cells when it creates the pivot table.

In general, it's safest to place a pivot table on its own new worksheet. If you restructure the pivot table, it can grow to overwrite other values on the sheet (Excel warns you before overwriting existing data).

**4** Click OK.

Excel inserts the new pivot table. The pivot table appears as an empty placeholder until you define the rows, columns, and values to use to summarize the source data. When you select a cell inside the pivot table, Excel displays the PivotTable Field List pane on the right, which lists all the columns in the source data.

If you chose to create a new worksheet, Excel gives the sheet a generic name (Sheet2 or whatever) and then places it before the worksheet that contains the source data. You can rename the new worksheet (double-click its worksheet tab) and then drag the tab left or right to reposition the worksheet.

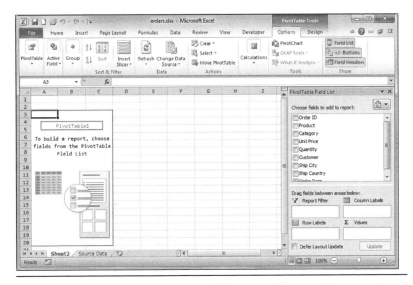

**Note:** Pivot tables created in Excel 97–2003 compatibility mode have a series of linked "drop fields here" boxes instead of a single pane. No worries: the instructions in this book still work for old-style pivot tables.

## Deleting a Pivot Table

A pivot table is a monolithic grid, meaning deletion is all-or-nothing. Excel won't let you insert or delete individual cells, rows, or columns in a pivot table.

### To delete a pivot table:

1 Select the entire pivot table.

 To select the entire pivot table, drag to select all the pivot table's cells (including headers). Or click anywhere in the pivot table and then choose PivotTable Tools > Options tab > Actions group > Select arrow > Entire PivotTable.

2 Press Delete.

**Note:** Deleting a pivot table turns any of its associated pivot charts (Chapter 6) into standard charts that you can no longer pivot or update.

## Laying Out Pivot Tables

To lay out a pivot table, you use the **PivotTable Field List**. Drag columns, called **fields**, from the "Choose fields to add to report" list into any of the four boxes underneath. You can also select the checkbox next to a field; Excel will place it in a box depending on the field's data type (if Excel guesses wrong, drag the field to the correct box). Excel updates the pivot table dynamically as you add, rearrange, or remove fields.

The PivotTable Field List appears when you select any cell in a pivot table. If it doesn't appear, choose PivotTable Tools > Options tab > Show group > Field List.

**Note:** The examples in this book use the default view ("Fields Section and Areas Section Stacked") of the PivotTable Field List pane. To change the view, click 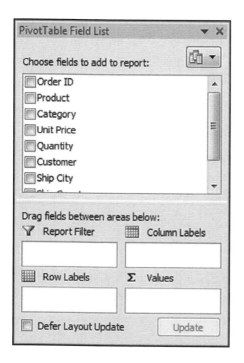 near the upper-right corner of the pane. The default view is designed for a small number of fields. The other views are optimized for adding, removing, or rearranging many fields.

A pivot table has four areas:

*Values*

> These fields are the numerical values for which you want to display sums, averages, counts, and other statistics. For example, you can drag the Unit Price field here to calculate price statistics. (If you drag a non-numerical field to Values, only counts are calculated.) For details, see Chapter 4.

*Row Labels*

> These fields group the data into levels, one level per row. For example, you can drag the Category field here to show product categories (Beverages, Condiments, and so on).

*Column Labels*

> These fields also create levels, one level per column. You can use both Row Labels and Column Labels to divide your data in multiple ways in the same pivot table. For example, if you drag Ship Country to Row Labels, Category to Column Labels, and Quantity to Values, then the pivot table divides sales figures into rows by country and columns by product category (answering the question, "Which types of products sell best in each country?").

*Report Filter*

> These fields limit the data displayed in the pivot table. For example, to show a breakdown of U.S.-only sales by product category, drag Ship Country to Report Filter and then configure the filter to show only "USA" values. For details, see "Report Filters" in Chapter 5.

## Rearranging (Pivoting) a Pivot Table

In the PivotTable Field List pane, you can remove or move fields at any time to rearrange (pivot) the pivot table.

### To remove a field from a pivot table:

- Drag the field from any box out of the PivotTable Field List pane (the mouse pointer changes to an × as you drag).

  *or*

Click the field in a box and then choose Remove Field from the pop-up menu.

*or*

Clear the checkbox next to the field name in the field list.

### To move a field from one area to another:

- Drag the field from one box to another.

  *or*

  Click the field in a box and then choose a "Move to" command from the pop-up menu.

## Row or Column Label?

Choosing whether a field appears as a row or column label is a matter of formatting and readability (either way, the same data are displayed). Fields with long category names or many distinct values typically work better as row labels (as column labels, they stretch or proliferate columns). For example, the Product field works best as a row label; as a column label, the pivot table would be 77 columns wide (Alice Mutton, Aniseed Syrup,..., Zaanse koeken) and hard to read and print.

## Moving a Pivot Table

You can move a pivot table to a new worksheet or an existing one. Select any cell in the pivot table and then choose PivotTable Tools > Options tab > Actions group > Move PivotTable.

## PivotTable Options

You can change the most common pivot-table settings by using the ribbon and PivotTable Field List pane, but you can find many others in the PivotTable Options dialog box. To open it, right-click any cell in the pivot table and then choose PivotTable Options (or choose PivotTable Tools > Options tab > PivotTable group > Options). Settings made in this dialog box apply to only the active pivot table.

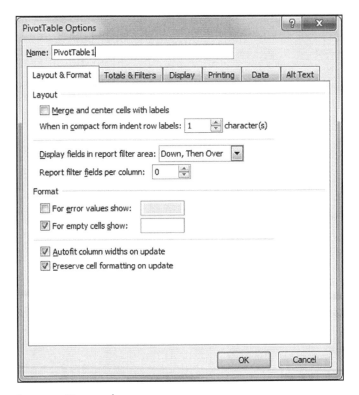

## Layout Examples

The following example creates a summary that compares products and shipping locations. The result is a **two-dimensional** pivot table. Most pivot tables seen in practice are two-dimensional, meaning that they summarize two different fields.

---

**Note:** If you're using the sample workbook (page 1) to follow along, the look of your pivot tables depends on which report layout (compact, outline, or tabular form) you choose. For details, see "Formatting Pivot Tables" later in this chapter.

---

### To compare products and shipping locations:

1  If necessary, create a new pivot table (page 4).

2  In the PivotTable Field List pane, drag the Product field to the Row Labels box underneath.

Excel fills in all the product names from the source data from top to bottom (in alphabetical order), one product per row.

**3** Drag the Ship Country field to the Column Labels box.

Excel fills in all the country names from the source data from left to right (in alphabetical order), one country per column.

**4** Drag the Quantity field to the Values box.

This step chooses which data to examine. Excel fills the pivot table with the numbers of products that were ordered by customers in various countries. The default calculation for pivot tables is the sum of each field in the Values box (note the label "Sum of Quantity" in the Values box). In this example, each value is the total number of units of a specific product shipped to a specific country.

Pivot tables also calculate subtotals and grand totals. To see them, scroll to rightmost or bottommost end of the pivot table. The grand total is in the bottom-right corner.

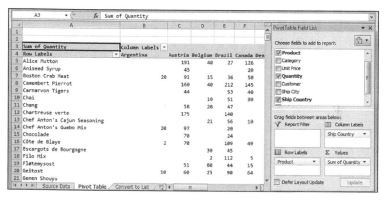

You can also *nest* fields by placing them together in the Row Labels or Column Labels box. For example, starting with an empty pivot table, drag Product to the Row Labels box, drag Ship Country to the same box (placing it under Product), and then drag Quantity to the Values box. The order of fields within a box determines their nesting order in the pivot table (here, Ship Country is nested within Product). For details, see Chapter 2.

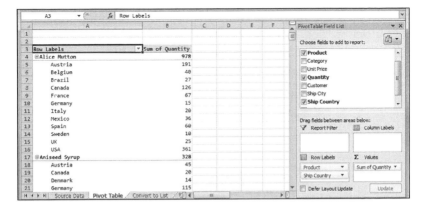

A **one-dimensional** pivot table has a single field in either the Column Labels or Row Labels box (but not both). For example, starting with an empty pivot table, drag Product to the Row Labels box and then drag Quantity to the Values box. The resulting pivot table simply totals the number of units sold by product.

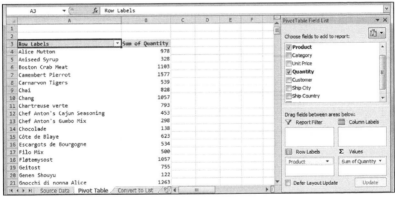

## Refreshing Pivot Tables

Unlike formulas, charts, and most other elements in Excel, pivot tables don't auto-update when the underlying data change. If you change the source data, the pivot table can show out-of-date totals. A **refresh** makes Excel scan the source data and recalculate the pivot table.

## To refresh a pivot table manually:

- Right-click the pivot table and then choose Refresh.

  *or*

  Select any cell in the pivot table and then press Alt+F5.

  *or*

  Select any cell in the pivot table and then choose PivotTable Tools > Options tab > Data group > Refresh (or click Refresh All to refresh all pivot tables in the workbook).

## To autorefresh a pivot table when you open a workbook:

- Select any cell in the pivot table and then choose PivotTable Tools > Options tab > PivotTable group > Options > Data tab > select "Refresh data when opening the file".

---

**Note:** A refresh can take a long time depending on the amount of source data, the complexity of the pivot table, the speed of your computer, and other factors. After starting a refresh, you can review its status or cancel it at any time by choosing Refresh Status or Cancel Refresh from the Refresh menu.

---

## Autoformatting on Refresh

If a pivot table becomes misformatted when you refresh it, select the "Autofit column widths on update" and "Preserve cell formatting on update" checkboxes on the Layout & Format tab in the PivotTable Options dialog box (PivotTable Tools > Options tab > PivotTable group > Options).

## Deferring Updates

By default, Excel regenerates a pivot table—and any associated pivot charts (Chapter 6)—every time that you drag a field to or from a box in the PivotTable Field List pane. If pivot-table calculations involve a large data source or many nested fields (Chapter 2), then refresh can be intolerably slow.

To disable autorefresh, select the Defer Layout Update checkbox at the bottom of the PivotTable Field List pane. When this setting is turned on, Excel doesn't refresh the pivot table as you change it. To see the effects of your changes, refresh the pivot table manually by clicking the Update button (next to the checkbox), or clear the Defer Layout Update checkbox to go back to automatic refresh.

## Disabling Undo for Large Data Sources

If a pivot table is linked to a large data source, then undoing refresh operations slows performance because Excel must track and recalculate the pivot table's prior states. You can turn off undo for time-consuming refreshes without affecting minor refreshes or other types of undo operations. Choose File tab > Options > Advanced (on the left) > General section. To turn off undo for large data sources, lower the undo threshold for "Disable undo for PivotTables with at least this number of data source rows (in thousands)". To disable undo for all pivot tables, set this value to zero.

On the other hand, you can enable undo for *all* pivot tables (which is convenient but can significantly slow Excel): clear "Disable undo for large PivotTable refresh operations to reduce refresh time".

## Formatting Pivot Tables

When you select a cell in a pivot table, the ribbon sprouts two new tabs under the PivotTable Tools heading. These tabs are similar to the ones that appear when you select a chart, table, or picture.

The PivotTable Tools > Options tab accesses advanced features like custom calculations, filtering, and pivot charts (covered in later chapters). The PivotTable Tools > Design tab changes the appearance of pivot tables.

The Design tab has three groups:

*PivotTables Styles*

Click a style to change the colors and shading of the pivot table. The colors come from the workbook theme that you're using. To use a different set of colors, choose Page Layout tab > Themes group > Themes.

*PivotTables Style Options*

If you don't want shading to alternate from one row or column to the next, clear the Banded Rows or Banded Columns checkboxes. If you don't want to apply the style formatting to headers, clear the Row Headers or Column Headers checkboxes.

*Layout*

Choose a preset option that controls spacing and subtotals.

*Grand Totals.* Show or hide the totals at the end of each row or column.

*Subtotals.* Show or hide subtotals at the end of each level. This setting applies only if fields are nested; that is, the Row Labels or Column Labels box contains more than one field. Otherwise, the levels' "subtotals" are actually grand totals.

*Report Layout.* By default, pivot tables are shown in **compact form**: all row labels are merged into a single column, and each column just wide enough to fit that column's widest entry. In **outline form**, each row label gets its own column, and each column is as wide as the widest column in the whole pivot table (which occupies much more space). **Tabular form** is like outline form but shows subtotals (extra rows) at the bottom of each level or group. You can also **repeat labels** to show values of nested fields in all row and column labels.

*Blank Rows.* Show or hide blank lines between levels or groups. This option applies only if the Row Labels section has more than one field.

**Tip:** If you're going to copy or export a pivot table from Excel to another program (such as a database or accounting program), then use outline form and turn on repeating labels.

## Showing a Value's Source Data

If you spot a trend, unexpected relationship, or an outlier (suspicious observation) in a pivot table, you can easily "drill down" to see exactly how the value was calculated. To do so, double-click any value cell in a pivot table. Excel creates a new worksheet containing copies of only the records that were used to calculate that cell's value. This method is superior to the tedious alternative: switching to the worksheet that contains the original source data and then searching for the corresponding records.

The following pivot table shows how product categories (rows) perform in each country (columns). Double-click cell B5…

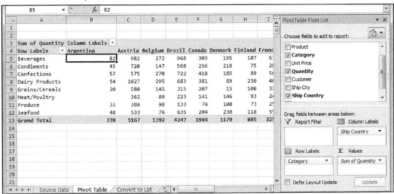

…and Excel adds a worksheet containing copies of the seven records whose Quantity values were summed to produce Argentine beverage sales.

After you finish examining the data, you can delete the worksheet that contains the copied records (right-click the worksheet tab at the bottom of the window and then choose Delete). The original source data aren't touched when you delete the copy.

If you spot an error in the copied records, you must flip to the original source data to fix it. Obvious, yes, but it's easy to absentmindedly change the *copied* records and then wonder why the refreshed pivot table doesn't change.

## Changing a Pivot Table's Source Data

If you add rows to the bottom of a range of source data, you can redefine the pivot table's source data to include those rows. Select any cell in the pivot table and then choose PivotTable Tools > Options tab > Data group > Change Data Source.

---

**Note:** If the source data are in an Excel table (Insert tab > Tables group > Table), then you don't have to change the range—newly added rows are displayed automatically when you refresh the pivot table.

---

# 2

# Nesting Fields

You've already seen examples of one- and two-dimensional pivot tables (page 10), but Excel doesn't limit the number of fields in a pivot table.

### To add additional (nested) fields to a pivot table:

1   Select any cell in the pivot table.

Excel shows the PivotTable Field List pane.

2   In the PivotTable Field List pane, drag fields from the "Choose fields to add to report" list to the Row Labels or Column Labels boxes underneath.

Each time you add a new field, Excel subdivides, or nests, the current fields. The order of fields within a box determines their nesting order in the pivot table.

For example, consider a pivot table with the settings:

**Row Labels:** Product, Ship Country
**Column Labels:** <empty>
**Values:** Quantity (summarized by Sum)
**Report Filter:** <empty>

Each row in this pivot table shows the total units of a specific product shipped to a specific country.

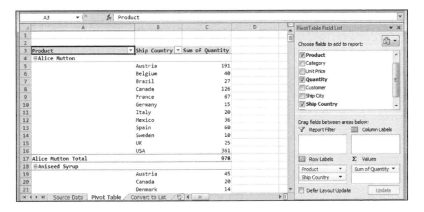

Excessive nesting can make a pivot table uninformative or unwieldy. If the number of rows in a pivot table is close to the number of rows in the underlying source data, then that pivot table isn't actually a summary. Another sign of an overnested pivot table is an excessive number of empty cells (wasted space).

For example, consider a pivot table with the settings:

**Row Labels:** Category, Order Date
**Column Labels:** Ship Country
**Values:** Quantity (summarized by Sum)
**Report Filter:** <empty>

The rows in this pivot table are grouped by category and subdivided by order date. At 1605 rows (not counting subtotals or blank values), this pivot table isn't much smaller than the source data (2155 rows). The problem is that few orders fall on the same date. And when they do, they're usually for different product categories. Consequently, many rows show results for only a single order, rather than true totals. This pivot table is **sparse** (contains many empty cells) because each row is further broken up into columns by country.

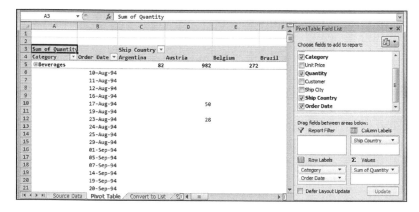

Nesting works best for *related* fields, such as Category and Product (each product falls in one category):

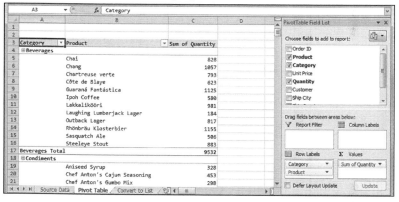

Or Ship Country and Ship City (each city is located in one country):

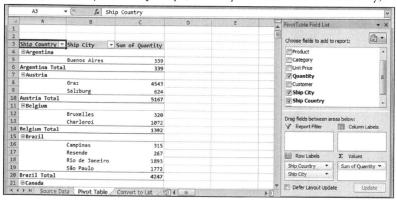

Make sure that you place the fields in the correct order in the Labels box; otherwise, you'll get silly results. For example, consider a pivot table with the settings:

**Row Labels:** Product, Category
**Column Labels:** <empty>
**Values:** Quantity (summarized by Sum)
**Report Filter:** <empty>

This pivot table groups the records by product and then subdivides the products by category, resulting in an unhelpful pivot table where each group contains a single subgroup (because each product falls in only one category). To fix this pivot table, swap the row labels.

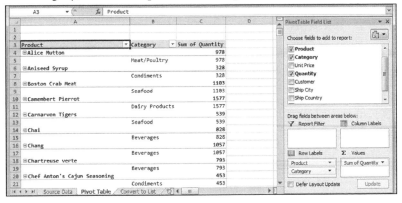

### To reorder fields in a pivot table:

**1** Select any cell in the pivot table.

Excel shows the PivotTable Field List pane.

**2** In the PivotTable Field List pane, drag fields up or down within a box, or click a field in a box and then choose Move Up or Move Down (or Move to Beginning or Move to End) from the pop-up menu.

# Showing and Hiding Levels

You can show (**expand**) or hide (**collapse**) individual levels in nested rows or columns, concealing the parts of a pivot table that you don't want to see. In a pivot table that nests Product within Category, for example, you can show only the products in a specific category and hide the rest.

### To show or hide specific levels:

- Click the plus (+) or minus (–) icon next to the level name in the pivot table (click again to toggle visibility).

   *or*

   Double-click the cell containing the level name (double-click again to toggle visibility).

   *or*

   Right-click the cell containing the level name and then choose Expand or Collapse from the Expand/Collapse submenu.

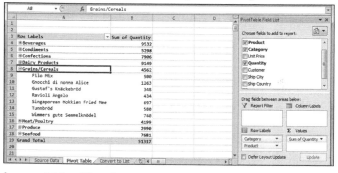

### To show or hide all levels:

- In the target field, right-click any cell containing a level name and then choose Expand Entire Field or Collapse Entire Field from the Expand/Collapse submenu.

   *or*

   In the target field, select any cell containing a level name and then choose PivotTable Tools > Options tab > Active Field group > Expand Entire Field or Collapse Entire Field.

If you try to expand an innermost nested level, Excel opens the Show Detail dialog box listing all the fields not currently showing. If you select a field and then click OK, Excel adds another nested field to the pivot table.

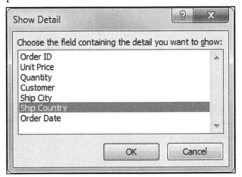

# 3

# Grouping Items

Pivot tables let you combine items into **groups**, which you can use to subset related values that can't be easily combined by sorting, filtering, or other means. Numbers, dates, times, and user-selected items can be grouped.

## Grouping by Selected Items

To create a custom group, select the items in the pivot table that you want to group, either by clicking or dragging, and then choose PivotTable Tools > Options tab > Group group > Group Selection (or right-click a selected cell and then choose Group from the shortcut menu).

---

**Tip:** To select adjacent cells, click the first cell and then Shift-click the last cell. To select nonadjacent cells, Ctrl-click each cell.

---

For example, start with a pivot table that has these settings in the Pivot-Table Field List pane:

**Row Labels:** Ship Country
**Column Labels:** <empty>
**Values:** Quantity (summarized by Sum)
**Report Filter:** <empty>

In the pivot table, Ctrl-click Canada, Mexico, and USA; right-click any selected item; and then choose Group.

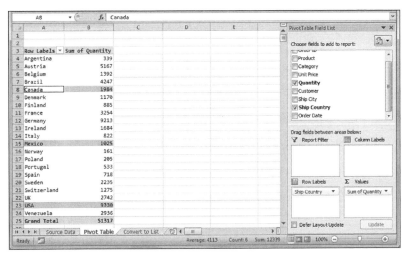

Replace the default group name (Group 1) with a meaningful name (North America). Excel also creates a new virtual field named Ship Country2 in the Row Labels box, which you can pivot on (for example, drag Ship Country2 to the Column Labels box). To remove the grouping, right-click the group name and then choose Ungroup.

| Row Labels | Sum of Quantity |
|---|---|
| ⊞ Argentina | 339 |
| ⊞ Austria | 5167 |
| ⊞ Belgium | 1392 |
| ⊞ Brazil | 4247 |
| ⊟ North America | |
| Canada | 1984 |
| Mexico | 1025 |
| USA | 9330 |
| ⊞ Denmark | 1170 |
| ⊞ Finland | 885 |
| ⊞ France | 3254 |
| ⊞ Germany | 9213 |
| ⊞ Ireland | 1684 |
| ⊞ Italy | 822 |
| ⊞ Norway | 161 |
| ⊞ Poland | 205 |
| ⊞ Portugal | 533 |
| ⊞ Spain | 718 |
| ⊞ Sweden | 2235 |
| ⊞ Switzerland | 1275 |
| ⊞ UK | 2742 |
| ⊞ Venezuela | 2936 |
| Grand Total | 51317 |

## Nested Groups

You can create any number of groups and even create nested groups (groups of groups). When you create nested groups, it's usually easiest to define the broadest (outermost) group first and then progress to the innermost groups.

| | A | B |
|---|---|---|
| 1 | | |
| 2 | | |
| 3 | Row Labels ▼ | Sum of Quantity |
| 4 | ⊟World | |
| 5 | ⊟Americas | |
| 6 | ⊟South America | |
| 7 | Argentina | 339 |
| 8 | Brazil | 4247 |
| 9 | Venezuela | 2936 |
| 10 | ⊟North America | |
| 11 | Canada | 1984 |
| 12 | Mexico | 1025 |
| 13 | USA | 9330 |
| 14 | ⊟Europe | |
| 15 | ⊟Europe | |
| 16 | Austria | 5167 |
| 17 | Belgium | 1392 |
| 18 | Denmark | 1170 |
| 19 | Finland | 885 |
| 20 | France | 3254 |
| 21 | Germany | 9213 |
| 22 | Ireland | 1684 |
| 23 | Italy | 822 |
| 24 | Norway | 161 |
| 25 | Poland | 205 |
| 26 | Portugal | 533 |
| 27 | Spain | 718 |
| 28 | Sweden | 2235 |
| 29 | Switzerland | 1275 |
| 30 | UK | 2742 |
| 31 | Grand Total | 51317 |

## Grouping by Time Periods

When a field contains dates or times, you can create groups that summarize data by time periods (hours, months, years, and so on). For example, you can use the Order Date field to summarize sales by month. Start with a pivot table that has these settings in the PivotTable Field List pane:

**Row Labels:** Order Date
**Column Labels:** <empty>
**Values:** Quantity (summarized by Sum)
**Report Filter:** <empty>

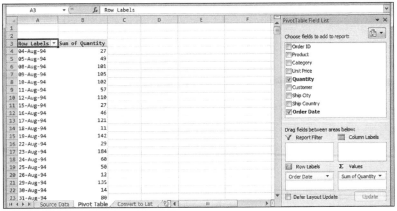

In the pivot table, right-click any cell in the Order Date (Row Labels) column and then select Group from the shortcut menu. The Grouping dialog box opens. In the By list, select Months and Years. Verify that the starting and ending dates are correct and then click OK.

The Order Date items in the pivot table are grouped by years and by months. Excel also creates a new virtual field named Years in the Row Labels box, which you can pivot on (for example, drag Years to the Column Labels box). To remove the grouping, right-click any cell in the Order Date (Row Labels) column and then choose Ungroup.

| | A | B |
|---|---|---|
| 1 | | |
| 2 | | |
| 3 | Row Labels ▼ | Sum of Quantity |
| 4 | ⊟1994 | |
| 5 | Aug | 1462 |
| 6 | Sep | 1322 |
| 7 | Oct | 1124 |
| 8 | Nov | 1669 |
| 9 | Dec | 1804 |
| 10 | ⊟1995 | |
| 11 | Jan | 2200 |
| 12 | Feb | 1951 |
| 13 | Mar | 2582 |
| 14 | Apr | 1622 |
| 15 | May | 2060 |
| 16 | Jun | 2164 |
| 17 | Jul | 1635 |
| 18 | Aug | 2054 |
| 19 | Sep | 1861 |
| 20 | Oct | 2343 |
| 21 | Nov | 2657 |
| 22 | Dec | 1878 |
| 23 | ⊟1996 | |
| 24 | Jan | 2682 |
| 25 | Feb | 3293 |
| 26 | Mar | 3288 |
| 27 | Apr | 4065 |
| 28 | May | 4957 |
| 29 | Jun | 644 |
| 30 | Grand Total | 51317 |

**Note:** If you select only Months (and not Years) in the list box, then months in different years are combined. The Aug item, for example, would show the combined quantities for 1994 and 1995 (the data stop in June, 1996).

## Grouping by Weeks

You can also group by week (or any fixed span of days). In the Grouping dialog box, select only Days (nothing else) in the By list and then type 7 in the "Number of days" box. Clear the "Starting at" checkbox and then adjust the start date to fall on the first day (typically, Sunday or Monday) of the first week of interest. If you like, adjust the end date too. Click OK.

Each row in the resulting pivot table shows the start and end dates of each week.

| ⊿ | A | B |
|---|---|---|
| 1 | | |
| 2 | | |
| 3 | Row Labels ▼ | Sum of Quantity |
| 4 | 8/1/1994 - 8/7/1994 | 76 |
| 5 | 8/8/1994 - 8/14/1994 | 475 |
| 6 | 8/15/1994 - 8/21/1994 | 347 |
| 7 | 8/22/1994 - 8/28/1994 | 335 |
| 8 | 8/29/1994 - 9/4/1994 | 378 |
| 9 | 9/5/1994 - 9/11/1994 | 254 |
| 10 | 9/12/1994 - 9/18/1994 | 236 |

# Grouping by Numbers

You can group by numbers to create a **frequency distribution**, where each entry in the pivot table contains the frequency (count) of the occurrences of values within a particular group or interval.

For example, start with a pivot table that has these settings in the Pivot-Table Field List pane:

**Row Labels:** Quantity
**Column Labels:** <empty>
**Values:** Quantity (summarized by Sum)
**Report Filter:** <empty>

The pivot table shows the quantity of units sold and the corresponding number of orders. The goal is to determine how many quantities are in each 10-point range (1–10, 11–20, and so on).

In the pivot table, right-click any cell in the Quantity (Row Labels) column and then select Group from the shortcut menu.

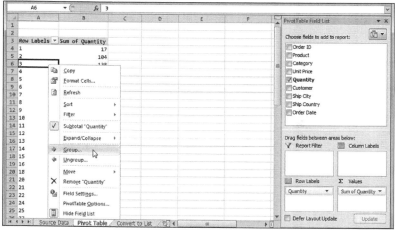

The Grouping dialog box opens. In the By box, type the size of the interval for each group (here, 10). Verify that the starting and ending points are correct and then click OK.

The Quantity items in the pivot table are grouped in uniform intervals (bins). The groups start at 1 and end at 130, in increments of 10. A column chart (Chapter 6) of a frequency distribution is a **histogram**. To remove the grouping, right-click any cell in the Quantity (Row Labels) column and then choose Ungroup.

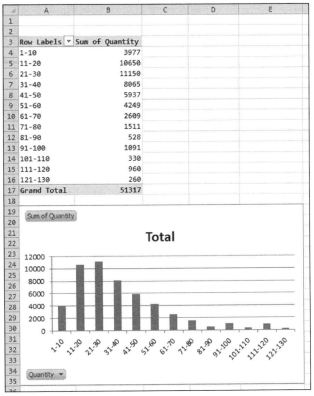

**Note:** By default, pivot tables don't display items with a count of zero. To make sure that your frequency distribution has no gaps between intervals, select any cell in the interval column and then choose PivotTable Tools > Options tab > Active Field group > Field Settings > Layout & Print tab > select "Show items with no data".

# 4

# Calculations and Custom Formulas

When you add a field to the Values box in the PivotTable Field List pane, Excel (in most cases) sums all the values in that field, but you can also calculate common statistics, do multiple calculations in the same pivot table, and create custom formulas.

## Calculating Common Statistics

Excel's preset calculations include common statistics: sum, count, average, maximum, percentage, rank, and so on.

### To choose a preset calculation:

1  Select any cell in the pivot table.

   Excel shows the PivotTable Field List pane.

2  In the PivotTable Field List pane, click the target field (for example, "Sum of Quantity") in the Values box and then choose Value Field Settings from the pop-up menu.

   The Value Field Settings dialog box opens.

**3**   In the "Summarize Values By" tab, choose a calculation in the list (Sum, Count, Average,...).

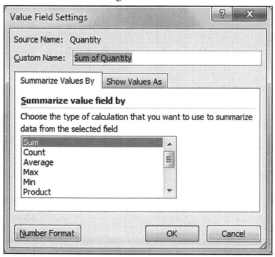

Alternatively, click the "Show Values As" tab to choose a more-complex calculation (percentage, difference, running total, rank, or index).

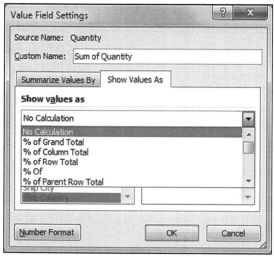

You can also change the default field name by typing a new name in the Custom Name box.

**4** To format the field's values, click Number Format, choose or define a new format, and then click OK.

You can change the number of decimal places, add a currency symbol, and so on.

**5** Click OK to close the Value Field Settings dialog box.

Excel refreshes the pivot table with the new calculations.

### Showing Zeros in Empty Cells

If the value of a pivot-table cell is zero, Excel shows it as an empty cell (inconsistent with non-pivot-table cells, which show zeros as zeros by default). To show zeros in a pivot table, right-click any cell in the pivot table and then choose PivotTable Options (or choose PivotTable Tools > Options tab > PivotTable group > Options). On the Layout & Format tab, clear the "For empty cells show" checkbox.

## Calculating Multiple Statistics

When you add multiple fields to the Values box, each field is calculated and shown in a separate column in the pivot table. To sum the Quantity and average the Unit Price, for example, drag both fields into the Values box and then follow the steps above to configure each field separately.

Similarly, you can do multiple calculations on the *same* field. To sum and average Quantity, for example, drag Quantity into the Values box twice and then configure the two Quantity fields separately.

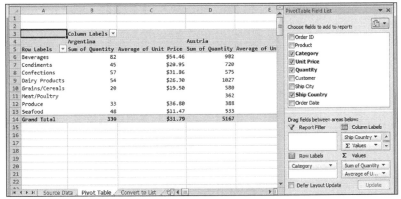

## Adding Custom Calculations

In addition to choosing a preset calculation, you can define a custom **calculated field** in a pivot table.

### To add a calculated field:

**1**  Select any cell in the pivot table.

**2**  Choose PivotTable Tools > Options tab > Calculations group > Fields, Items, & Sets > Calculated Field.

The Insert Calculated Field dialog box opens.

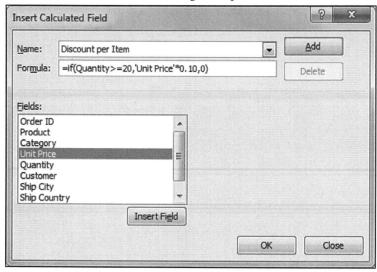

**3**  In the Name text box, type or paste a name for the new field.

**4**  In the Formula text box, enter the formula for this field.

The formula can use Excel's built-in operators and functions, or change or combine one or more of the fields in the Fields list. To insert a field name in the formula quickly, double-click the name in the list. If you manually type a field name that contains spaces or special characters, enclose the name in single quotes (for example, 'Unit Price').

5   Click OK.

In the PivotTable Field List pane, Excel adds the calculated field to the fields list and the Values box, so that it appears in the pivot table. Excel sums the formula for every row.

If you remove the custom field from the Values box to remove it from the pivot table, it remains in the fields list for later use. To permanently delete a custom field, select it from the Name drop-down list in the Insert Calculated Field dialog box (shown above) and then click Delete.

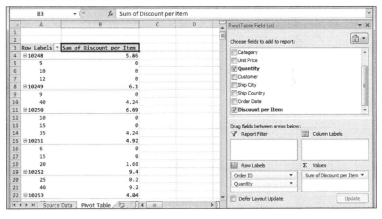

**Tip:** To list all calculated fields in a new worksheet, choose PivotTable Tools > Options tab > Calculations group > Fields, Items, & Sets > List Formulas.

## Troubleshooting Calculated Fields

Calculated fields have the following restrictions:

- A calculated-field formula can't refer to pivot-table grand totals or subtotals, nor can it refer to worksheet cells by address or by name.

- You can summarize a calculated field by only Sum.

- Because calculated-field formulas are always applied against the *sum* of the underlying data, Excel calculates data fields, subtotals, and grand totals before evaluating the calculated field.

In nontrivial formulas, the last restriction can cause unexpected results because the sum of products (generally) isn't equal to the product of sums. In the example above, the calculated field returns a 10 percent per-item price discount when a customer orders 20 or more units of a particular item, and no (zero) discount otherwise. In the resulting pivot table, the individual Quantity calculations are correct but the subtotals for each Order ID aren't what you'd expect (because Excel sums all an order's quantities *before* determining whether discounts apply). Another common trap: if you create a calculated field named Revenue with the formula =`'Unit Price' * Quantity`, Excel sums the prices, sums the quantities, and then multiplies the two sums—which is *not* what you want.

Sadly, there's no way to fix this problem, but there are a few (somewhat unsatisfying) workarounds for when you want sum-of-products and Excel is giving you product-of-sums:

- Add a column (field) to the underlying source data. In the sample workbook, for example, you can add a revenue formula to column J in the Source Data worksheet: type *Revenue* in cell J1, type =`D2*E2` in cell J2 (Unit Price × Quantity), and then fill down (Ctrl+D) the J2 formula to the end of the table.

- Copy (Ctrl+C) and paste values (Ctrl+Alt+V) from the pivot table to work with independently elsewhere in the workbook.

- Write formulas outside the pivot table. You might want to turn off the GETPIVOTDATA function (page 63) when you write formulas that refer to a pivot table (PivotTable Tools > Options tab > PivotTable group > Options arrow > Generate GetPivotData toggle).

- Turn off grand totals and subtotals in the pivot table (PivotTable Tools > Design tab > Layout group) and then calculate your own totals outside the pivot table.

# 5

# Filtering Data

If a pivot table displays too much detail, you can **filter** (restrict) it to show only part of the source data. Excel offers three types of filtering: report filters, slicers, and group filters.

---

**Note:** If a pivot table's data source is a table (Insert tab > Tables group > Table), then any filters that you apply directly to the table have no effect on linked pivot tables. To filter data from a pivot table, you must use one of the following methods.

---

## Report Filters

Report filters let you filter out data so that a pivot table uses only rows of interest in the source data. For example, start with a pivot table that has these settings in the PivotTable Field List pane:

**Row Labels:** Category
**Column Labels:** Ship City
**Values:** Quantity (summarized by Sum)
**Report Filter:** <empty>

To create a summary for only specific countries, drag the field Ship Country to the Report Filter box. The report filter field appears just above the pivot table. (If you use more than one report filter, each appears in a separate row.) To set the filter, click the drop-down arrow ▾ in the field box and then choose the countries that you want to display. To find an item, scroll the list or type the first few characters of its name in the Search box. To filter for several items at the same time, turn on the Select Multiple Items checkbox and then select the desired items. When you're done, click OK.

---

**Tip:** To control how report filter fields are arranged in rows and columns, select any cell in the pivot table and then choose PivotTable Tools > Options tab > PivotTable group > Options > Layout & Format tab.

---

Excel uses checked items to create the pivot table, and ignores unchecked items. To quickly remove a report filter, choose the first item in the report filter list: "(All)".

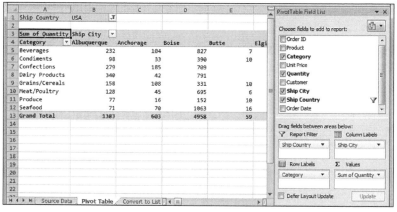

**Note:** Any fields that you use for report filtering *can't* also be used for grouping (Chapter 3). For example, if you filter by Ship Country, you can't also group by Ship Country. This restriction doesn't apply to slicers (covered next) and group filters (page 48).

## Slicers

Slicers offer about the same features as report filters (page 41), but in "dashboard" format. Each slicer has its own floating window, which you can format and drag around the main Excel window.

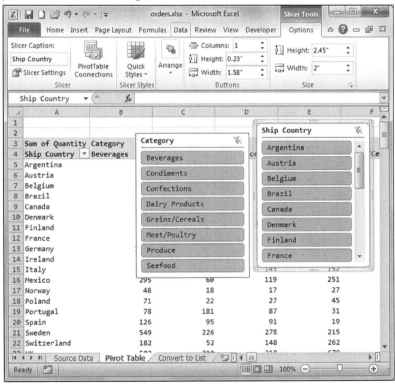

In contrast to report filters, slicers offer fast one-click filtering, and can filter and group on the same field. However, slicers tend to clutter your display with floating windows and don't work well with fields that have many distinct values (which cause long scrolling distances). Also, slicers, like report filters, are less powerful than group filters (page 48).

**To create a slicer:**

1 Select any cell in the pivot table.

2 Choose PivotTable Tools > Options tab > Sort & Filter group > Insert Slicer.

The Insert Slicers dialog box opens, listing all the fields in the pivot table (except custom fields, described on page 38).

3 Select the checkbox of each field that you want to use for filtering.

Fields that have a small number of unique values make the best slicers because they fit well in a floating slicer window. Good choices: Category and Ship Country. Middling choices: Product and Customer. Poor choices: Unit Price and Order Date.

4 Click OK.

Excel adds a separate floating window for each slicer.

**5** Move or resize the floating slicer windows as desired.

To move a slicer, point to a border (the pointer turns into a four-way arrow) and then drag. To resize a slicer, point to a corner or the middle of an edge (the pointer turns into a two-way arrow) and then drag.

**6** Use the slicer window to apply filtering.

The slicer window lists all the unique values in a field, each value appearing as a separate button. The buttons of *visible* values are shaded. No filtering is in effect in a newly created slicer window, so every button is shaded.

To filter to a single value, click its button.

To filter to multiple values, hold down the Ctrl key while you click each button. (To select a range of contiguous values, click the first button and then Shift-click the last button.)

To clear filtering (show everything for the field), click the funnel-X icon in the upper-right corner of the slicer window. Keyboard shortcut: Alt+C.

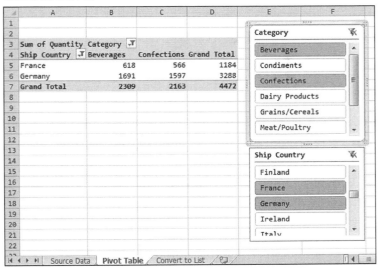

**7** (Optional) Format the slicer.

To change the button colors, choose Slicer Tools > Options tab > Slicer Styles gallery.

To expand or compact the slicer window, choose Slicer Tools > Options tab > Buttons group > change the Columns, Height, and Width values. The following figure shows a three-column slicer window with custom button colors.

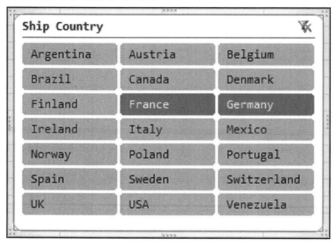

To change the window title, choose Slicer Tools > Options tab > Slicer group > Slicer Caption box. To hide the window title, choose Slicer Tools > Options tab > Slicer group > Slicer Settings > clear "Display header".

To sort a slicer's values, right click the slicer window and then choose a Sort command from the shortcut menu.

To remove a slicer, click it and then press Delete (or right-click it and then choose the Remove command from the shortcut menu).

## Custom Slicer Styles

You can create custom slicer styles to reuse with as many slicers as you want.

### To create a custom slicer style:

**1** Choose Slicer Tools > Options tab > Slicer Styles group. Click the drop-down arrow 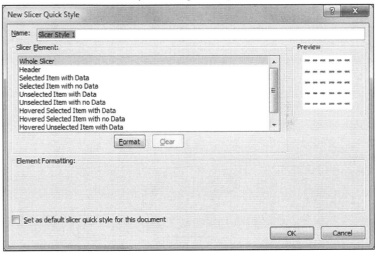 and then choose New Slicer Style.

The New Slicer Quick Style dialog box opens.

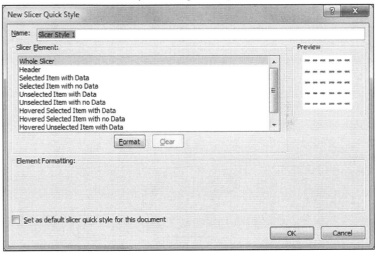

**2** In the Name box, type a name for the new slicer style.

**3** In the Slicer Element list, select an element.

Each element defines how a specific part of the slicer looks in a specific state. "Whole Slicer" formats the entire slicer and "Header" formats only the slicer's window title. The specialized elements below "Header" format how an item looks when it's selected, when it's hovered over by the pointer, and when there's no corresponding data for that value in the pivot table.

**4** Click Format to format the selected element.

The Format Slicer Element dialog box opens. Change the font, border, and fill as desired and then click OK.

**5**   To format other elements in the slicer, repeat steps 3 and 4.

**6**   Click OK to create the style.

The custom style appears in the Slicer Styles gallery. You can apply it to any slicer, or right-click it to modify, delete, or duplicate it.

## Group Filters

Group filters—more powerful than report filters (page 41) and slicers (page 43)—let you filter fields that you're using to group (Chapter 3) a pivot table to:

- Show or hide specific items (like report filters, except that you can't create report filters for grouping fields).

- Create complex conditions that subset data. For example, you can show or hide dates that fall in a specific time period or names that begin or end with a certain letter.

- Filter on multiple fields and configure them independently (Excel **additively** applies every filter at the same time).

The examples in this section use a pivot table with the following settings in the PivotTable Field List pane:

**Row Labels:** Category, Product
**Column Labels:** Ship Country
**Values:** Quantity (summarized by Sum)
**Report Filter:** <empty>

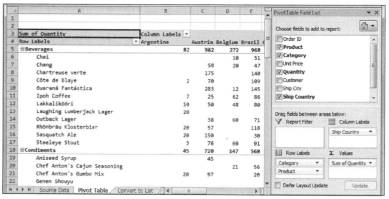

**To create a group filter:**

1  Click the drop-down arrow 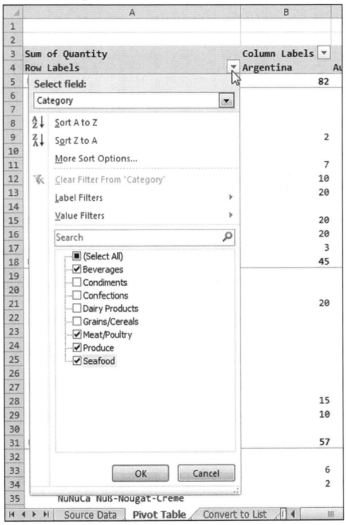 to the right of a Row Labels or Column Labels cell.

The filter list opens.

2  If you're grouping on multiple fields, choose a field from the "Select field" drop-down list at top.

**3** Set the desired options in the filter list and then click OK.

To show or hide specific items, select or clear their checkboxes. To find an item, scroll the list or type the first few characters of its name in the Search box.

To show or hide items that contain specific text, begin or end with a certain letter, and so on, choose an option from the Label Filters submenu. For example, to show only items that begin with "U", choose Label Filters > Begins With and then type *U* in the dialog box that opens.

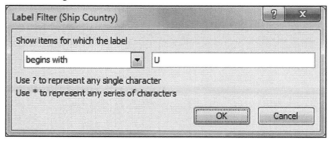

To show or hide calculated values based on numerical criteria (less than, greater than, Top 10, and so on), choose an option from the Value Filters submenu. For example, to show only items less than 500, choose Value Filters > Less Than and then type *500* in the dialog box that opens.

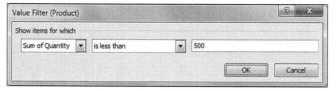

To sort items in ascending, descending, or custom order, choose a Sort command.

To remove a filter (show everything for the field), choose the Clear Filter command. If you have multiple filters, you must remove each one separately. To remove them all at once (and show all data), choose PivotTable Tools > Options tab > Actions group > Clear > Clear Filters.

**4** To filter by other grouping fields, repeat the preceding steps for each row label or column label.

## Filtering Nested Fields

Label filters and value filters can get tricky when you work with nested fields (Chapter 2). For example, the effect of the Value Filters > Less Than > 500 command differs depending on whether you apply it to the Product or Category field (recall that Product is nested within Category in this example). Applied to Product, the pivot table shows products that sold fewer than 500 units (as you'd expect). Applied to Category, only categories with sales fewer than 500 units across *all* their products appear. Because every category has sales greater than 500 units in the current example, the filter hides every category and shows an empty pivot table (which is correct logically but might not be what you'd expect).

Note that if you apply a filter to a row field (Category or Products, in this example), your column fields (Ship Country) have no effect. Likewise, row filters don't affect column filters.

# 6 Charting Pivot Tables

You can create charts based on the data in a pivot table. Pivot charts work the same as standard charts, but you may want to first filter a pivot table (Chapter 5) or remove excessive nesting (Chapter 2) to avoid creating charts with too many data series, which are hard to interpret and slow to refresh. Simple chart types like column and line charts work best (avoid 3-D effects, color gradients, gridlines, and other chartjunk).

---

**Note:** Pivot charts, like pivot tables, are dynamic. As you drag fields in the PivotTable Field List from one area to another, Excel automatically refreshes (page 12) the pivot table and pivot chart.

---

## Creating Pivot Charts

You insert a pivot chart on a worksheet in the same way that you insert a standard chart.

### To create a pivot chart:

1   Select any cell in the pivot table.

2   Choose PivotTable Tools > Options tab > Tools group > PivotChart.

    The Insert Chart dialog box opens.

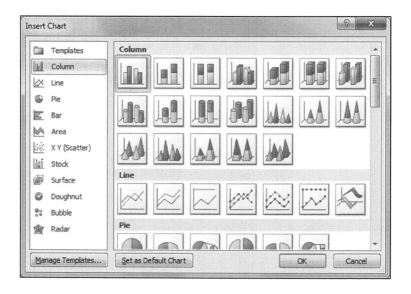

**3** Select the type of chart that you want and then click OK.

The pivot chart appears on the worksheet.

The following 100% Stacked Column chart shows Quantity by Category and Ship Country. Each color-coded bar is subdivided by country (denoted by the legend). The pivot table is filtered to show only a few categories and countries.

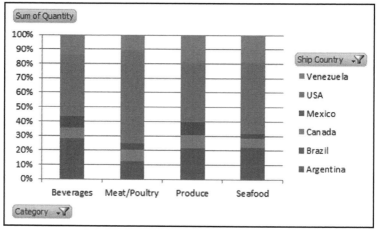

## Differences from Standard Charts

Most of what you can do with standard charts, you can also do with pivot charts, except for the following differences.

*Some chart types are prohibited*

Pivot charts can't be xy (scatter), stock, or bubble charts.

*Pivot to swap row–column orientation*

You can't use the Select Data Source dialog box to switch the row-column orientation of a pivot chart. Instead, pivot (swap) the fields in the Row Labels and Column Labels boxes to achieve the same effect.

*Chart data range is defined differently*

A standard chart is linked directly to worksheet cells, whereas a pivot chart is linked to a specific pivot table. You can't use the Select Data Source dialog box to change a pivot chart's data range.

*Some formatting isn't preserved on refresh*

Trendlines, data labels, error bars, and other changes to data sets are lost when you refresh the linked pivot table (page 12). Standard charts, in contrast, don't lose their formatting when their source data recalculates.)

## Customizing Pivot Charts

You have several ways to manipulate and customize a pivot chart.

*Format it*

When you select (click) a pivot chart, the ribbon sprouts new tabs under the PivotChart Tools heading. These tabs, similar to the Chart Tools tabs for standard charts, change the formatting and layout of the chart, and configure chart elements like titles, axes, and gridlines.

*Move it*

Excel places each pivot chart in a floating box. To move a chart, drag it (click an empty area of the chart to drag, or you may accidently drag or select only part of the chart). To move a chart to a new or different worksheet, click the chart and then choose PivotChart

Tools > Design tab > Location group > Move Chart. Alternatively, click the chart, press Ctrl+X (Home > Cut), switch to the target worksheet, and then press Ctrl+V (Home > Paste).

*Apply group filters*

You can apply group filters (page 48) directly on a pivot chart. Click one of the field buttons on the chart to show a drop-down list of filtering options. It makes no difference whether you set the filtering options on the chart or on the pivot table itself. If these buttons clutter your chart, you can hide them: choose PivotChart Tools > Analyze tab > Show/Hide group > Field Buttons.

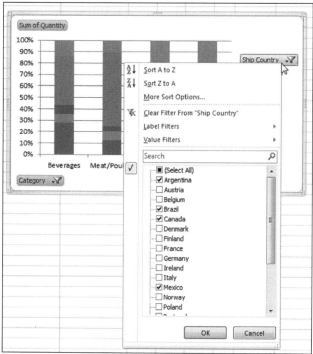

**Note:** When you click a pivot chart, the section names in the PivotTable Field List change to reflect which parts of the pivot table are used to create the chart. The Row Labels section becomes Axis Fields (chart categories) and the Column Labels section becomes Legend Fields (chart series).

# 7

# Tricks with Pivot Tables

Excel's arsenal of pivot-table features offers a few nonobvious ways to solve common problems.

## Creating a Frequency Tabulation

You can use a pivot table to quickly create a frequency tabulation for a single column of data. For example, in the sample workbook (page 1), switch to the Source Data worksheet, select the Ship Country column (click the H column heading), choose Insert tab > Tables group > PivotTable, and then create the pivot table (page 4). In the Pivot-Table Field List, drag the Ship Country field into the Row Labels box and then drag it again into the Values box. The resulting pivot table tallies the number of times that each country appears in the column. You can group, filter, and chart this tabulation as you would any pivot table. See also "Grouping by Numbers" in Chapter 3.

# Unlinking a Pivot Table from its Source Data

Excel doesn't provide a direct way to "unlink" a pivot table from its source data, but you can create an unlinked copy of a pivot table in a few steps (handy if you want to send someone a pivot table summary report but not its underlying data).

**To create an unlinked copy of a pivot table:**

1 Select the entire pivot table.

   To select the entire pivot table, drag to select all the pivot table's cells. Or click anywhere in the pivot table and then choose Pivot-Table Tools > Options tab > Actions group > Select arrow > Entire PivotTable.

2 Press Ctrl+C (Home > Copy).

3 Choose Home tab > Clipboard group > Paste arrow > Values.

   Excel replaces the pivot table by its values, but without formatting.

4 In the Home tab > Clipboard group, click the dialog box launcher icon ▣ in the bottom-right corner of the group.

   The Office Clipboard pane opens.

5 In the Office Clipboard pane (with the unlinked pivot table still selected), click the item that corresponds to the pivot table copy operation. That is, the most-recent action (unless you did something else in Office after the copy).

   Excel restores the original formatting in the unlinked pivot table. You can close the Office Clipboard pane.

# Converting a Summary Table to a List

If you have a two-dimensional summary table (an ordinary range of cells—not a pivot table), you can reverse the usual pivot-table procedure by converting the summary table to a list. Data in list form can be easier to sort, filter, and update than data in summary form.

To convert a summary to a list, you must first add the PivotTable and PivotChart Wizard command to your Quick Access toolbar. Excel still supports this wizard, but it's hidden by default.

### To access the PivotTable and PivotChart wizard:

1 Right-click the Quick Access toolbar (at the upper left of the Excel window) and then choose Customize Quick Access Toolbar from the shortcut menu.

   The Excel Options dialog box opens to the Quick Access Toolbar tab.

2 In the "Choose commands from" drop-down list, choose "Commands Not in the Ribbon".

3 Scroll down the list (on the left) and then select PivotTable and PivotChart Wizard.

4 Click Add.

5 Click OK.

   The PivotTable and PivotChart Wizard icon 🗔 appears in the Quick Access toolbar.

The following example works for the specific summary table shown below, but you can easily modify the steps to work with your data.

### To convert a summary table to a list:

1 Select any cell in the summary table.

| B2 | | ▼ | $f_x$ | 200 | |
|---|---|---|---|---|---|
| ◢ | A | B | C | D | |
| 1 | | North America | South America | Europe | |
| 2 | Q1 | 200 | 180 | 91 | |
| 3 | Q2 | 114 | 90 | 145 | |
| 4 | Q3 | 295 | 60 | 119 | |
| 5 | Q4 | 48 | 18 | 17 | |

2 In the Quick Access toolbar, click the PivotTable and PivotChart Wizard icon 🗔.

   The PivotTable and PivotChart Wizard dialog box opens.

**3** Select "Multiple consolidation ranges" and then click Next.

**4** Select "I will create the page fields" and then click Next.

**5** Specify the range of the summary table in the Range box (here, A1:D5), click Add, and then click Next.

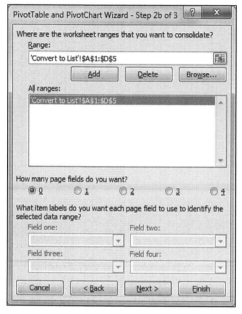

**6** Specify a target location for the pivot table and then click Finish.

Excel creates a pivot table from the summary table and shows the PivotTable Field List.

**7** In the PivotTable Field List, clear the checkboxes for the fields named Row and Column.

The pivot table shows a single field (Sum of Value), containing the sum of all the values in the table.

| | A | B | C | D | E | F |
|---|---|---|---|---|---|---|
| 1 | | North America | South America | Europe | | Sum of Value |
| 2 | Q1 | 200 | 180 | 91 | | 1377 |
| 3 | Q2 | 114 | 90 | 145 | | |
| 4 | Q3 | 295 | 60 | 119 | | |
| 5 | Q4 | 48 | 18 | 17 | | |

**8**  Double-click the cell that contains the total.

Excel creates a new worksheet that shows the original summary data in list form. Every value in the original summary table is converted to a row, which also contains the value's corresponding row and column labels. You can change the default column headings (Row, Column, and Value) to meaningful names.

| | A | B | C |
|---|---|---|---|
| 1 | Row ▼ | Column ▼ | Value ▼ |
| 2 | Q1 | North America | 200 |
| 3 | Q1 | South America | 180 |
| 4 | Q1 | Europe | 91 |
| 5 | Q2 | North America | 114 |
| 6 | Q2 | South America | 90 |
| 7 | Q2 | Europe | 145 |
| 8 | Q3 | North America | 295 |
| 9 | Q3 | South America | 60 |
| 10 | Q3 | Europe | 119 |
| 11 | Q4 | North America | 48 |
| 12 | Q4 | South America | 18 |
| 13 | Q4 | Europe | 17 |

# Controlling References to Pivot Table Cells

If you create a formula that refers to a cell within a pivot table, Excel automatically converts the cell reference to a GETPIVOTDATA function with arguments. For example:

```
=GETPIVOTDATA("Quantity", $A$3, "Category",
"Beverages", "Ship Country", "Argentina")
```

GETPIVOTDATA ensures that formulas still return the correct results even if you rearrange the pivot table (page 8). To avoid GETPIVOTDATA autoconversion, don't point to (click) the cell when you create the formula; instead, type the cell reference manually. To turn on or off GETPIVOTDATA autoconversion, choose PivotTable Tools > Options tab > PivotTable group > Options arrow > Generate GetPivotData toggle. Alternatively, choose File tab > Options > Formulas (on the left) > "Use GetPivotData functions for PivotTable references" checkbox.

# Replicating a Pivot Table for Report Filter Items

You can set up a pivot table and then replicate it for every distinct value of a report filter (page 41). This feature isn't popular because it generates multiple pivot tables when a single nested (Chapter 2) and filtered (Chapter 5) pivot table should suffice. It may be useful for generating separate tables or charts to paste in different slides in a presentation. Consider a pivot table with the settings:

**Row Labels:** Category
**Column Labels:** <empty>
**Values:** Quantity (summarized by Sum)
**Report Filter:** Ship Country

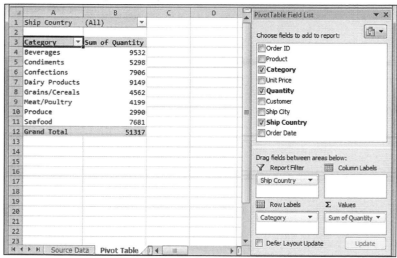

Choose PivotTable Tools > Options tab > PivotTable group > Options arrow > Show Report Filter Pages command. In the Show Report Filter Pages dialog box that opens, select Ship Country and then click OK. Excel replicates the pivot table for every country, creating a worksheet for each new pivot table (inspect the worksheet tabs at the bottom of the Excel window).

## Sorting a Pivot Table Manually

You can sort the rows or columns of a pivot table automatically by choosing PivotTable Tools > Options tab > Sort & Filter group, or sort them manually by dragging.

### To sort a pivot table manually:

1 In the pivot table, right-click any row or column label of the field that you want to sort and then choose Sort > More Sort Options > Manual > OK.

2 Select the label cell of the row or column that you want to move. If you want to move a group of adjacent rows or columns, drag to select multiple label cells.

3 Hover the pointer over the border of the selected label cell(s) until the pointer changes to a four-way arrow (called a *move pointer*). You may have to move the pointer slowly around the border until it changes to a move pointer.

4 Drag the selected row(s) or column(s) to another location within the pivot table.

As you drag, a thin line appears to show where the selection will land when dropped.

# Index

Made in the USA
San Bernardino, CA
26 March 2013